Britain
SINCE 1930

Gerald Haigh

Contents

	Page
Introduction	2
The Thirties	3
The Old Industries	3
The Depression	7
New Industries in the South	11
Transport	14
Fun and Holidays	18
The Second World War	21
Evacuation	22
Off to War	24
The Blitz	27
Rationing and the War Effort	30
Relaxing	34
The End of the War	36
Britain after the War	38
A Better Britain for All	40
You've Never Had It So Good	45
Railways and Travel	51
The 1960s	54
Glossary	55
Index	56

Introduction

Fred Haigh was born in 1903. He worked for a coal mine in a village near Sheffield. Fred met Jessie Ratcliffe, whose father was a coal miner, at a dance. They married in 1935. Their only child, Gerald, wrote this book. He was just two when the Second World War began in 1939. You will find out more about the Haigh family as you read this book.

Fred was lucky to have a job, because when this book begins in 1930, millions of people had no jobs. By the time the book ends in the 1960s, many incredible changes had taken place.

Our parents, grandparents and great grandparents are part of Britain's history. They lived during these times. Ask them what happened. They will enjoy remembering their past.

▲ Gerald Haigh and his family today.

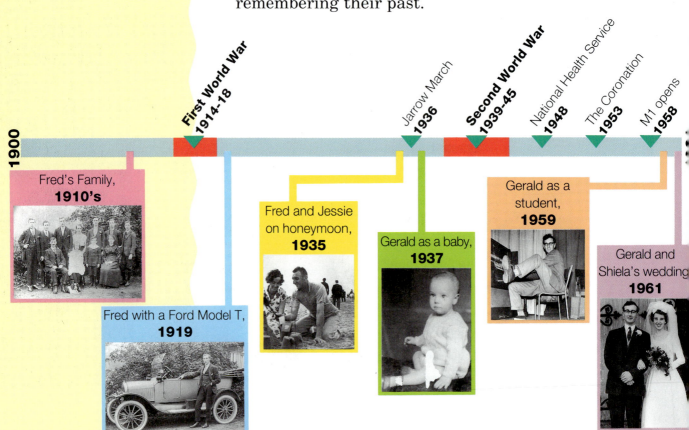

The Thirties

The Old Industries

When you exchange 25p for a nut bar, you **trade** with a shopkeeper. Countries trade, too. Today, Britain trades by selling **exports**, like Rolls Royce cars and Scotch whisky, to other countries. Exports help pay for the **imports** we buy from other countries, such as Spanish lemons, German VW cars or American wheat.

Before 1930, millions of British workers produced iron and steel, coal, cotton and ships. These '**old industries**' produced far more than we needed, so we exported the rest. Exports made Britain the world's richest country in Victorian times and paid for imported food and raw materials like cotton. People lost their jobs if factories did not export enough.

▶ Thousands of men worked in Britain's docks, loading and unloading exports and imports.

Coal mining

Have you seen a coal fire blazing in an open hearth? In 1930 most houses were heated like this.

3

▶ A fireman shovelling coal into a steam engine pulling the Night Mail, a special Post Office train. Coal once powered most ships and factory machines.

Deep below the fields of much of Britain, men toiled in the mines. British mines were small. British mine owners were slow to buy new machines, so their coal cost more to mine.

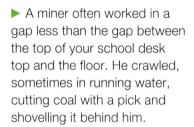

▶ A miner often worked in a gap less than the gap between the top of your school desk top and the floor. He crawled, sometimes in running water, cutting coal with a pick and shovelling it behind him.

Coal dust got into cuts and left blue scars. Mining was very dangerous. A miner explained,

My grandfather was blown to pieces by an explosion. They collected his remains with a rake and brought him home in a sack. My uncle worked in the mines until his back was broken by a fall of the roof.

Oil and electricity

By 1930 new factories had electric machines and more ships ran on oil. People burned less coal and British mine owners found it hard to export their expensive coal. They told the miners to work harder, to make the coal cheaper. They refused, and in 1926 the miners went on strike. Their leader said,

> Not a penny off the pay, not a second on the day.

The miners lost the long, bitter strike. They were forced back to work to do what the owners wanted. Thousands were sacked and became unemployed.

Cotton

Before 1930 thousands of Lancashire workers spun raw cotton into thread. Others wove the thread into cloth. Most cloth was exported and it was said that,

> Lancashire wove the home trade before breakfast... then wove for the world for the rest of the day.

India, Japan and China once bought most of their cloth from Britain. When they began making their own cheaper cloth, they stopped buying Lancashire cloth. Japan had more modern machines than Lancashire mills and paid its weavers less. A Lancashire girl earned almost ten times as much as a girl in Japan.

▼ Cotton weavers used clattering looms that were often 60 years old. Most spinners and weavers in the Lancashire mills were women or girls.

Cotton mills closed and many workers were sacked. Mill owners cut wages and tried to make people work harder. Weavers complained that they were forced to do twice as much work for only one worker's wages.

Shipbuilding

Shipyards in Belfast, Glasgow, and north east England once echoed to the din of men hammering steel. They built over half the world's steam cargo and passenger ships and hundreds of warships for navies all over the world. By the early 1930s few new warships were needed and many countries built their own cargo ships instead of buying British ships. Many British yards lay silent and over half the men had no work.

▼ Shipyard workers hammering red-hot rivets to join steel plates together. Can you see how the rivets were heated? A ship had thousands of plates joined like this.

a Discuss what is meant by the old industries. Make a design for the cover of a guide book about old industries in the 1930s. Include as many industries as you can in your design.

b Imagine you are a Health and Safety Inspector for the factory on page 5. Make a list of rules for the workers.

a Using an atlas and outline map of Britain, find out the main places where ships were built, coal mined and steel made.

The Depression

Millions of people all over the world had no jobs in the 1930s. Factories closed down or sacked workers if they could not sell enough of what they made. Ships lay idle, because as factories closed, countries traded less and ships had less cargo to carry. We call this time **the Depression**. In most countries it lasted until the Second World War.

A man in a book written in 1933 described unemployment,

> You fell into the habit of slouching, of putting your hands in your pockets; of glancing at people, ashamed of your secret, until you fancied everybody eyed you with suspicion. Your shabbiness betrayed you. You prayed for winter evenings and kindly darkness. Nothing to do with time; nothing to spend; nothing to do tomorrow nor the day after; nothing to wear; can't get married. A living corpse.

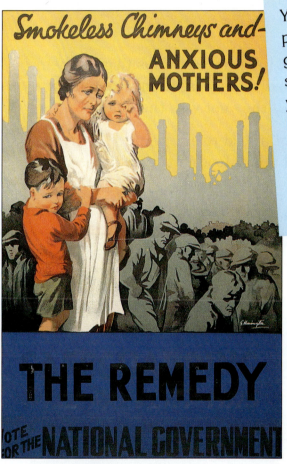

▲ A political poster protesting against poverty and unemployment.

▶ An unemployed Lancashire man. What is he wearing on his feet?

The government gave dole money to the unemployed. People hated the officials who always tried to cut their **dole** money. A man explained,

> An unemployed man was now at the mercy of officials [who] used to camp out in his front room, poking and prying into all the family's private affairs...if one of the children helped on a milk round for a few bob or ran errands or even was spotted wearing a new coat, the dole was adjusted [changed or reduced].

Some workers bought insurance stamps to give them more money if they lost their jobs. It only lasted six months. After that, all they got was the dole.

Food

Some people could not afford to eat properly. This is what two people said about food in the 1930s,

> Mrs D. of Liverpool lives entirely on tea and toast and margarine with an egg at weekends and a kipper twice a week.

> The other children are at school and thank God they got a meal there. Their breakfast is bread and margarine. Their tea bread and jam. But on Sunday we manage a meat dinner.

▶ This family's main meal was boiled fish, dry bread and sweet tea.

There were many poor people who lived in cramped houses with outside lavatories and no running hot water. This is how one person described slums in the north of England,

> Many houses contained only two rooms, one up and one down, joined by a rickety staircase rotting into holes. Windows are small and at two in the afternoon it is dark inside. When I touched the back walls my hand came away wet.

◀ London slums.

Hunger marches and Jarrow

The unemployed thought people with jobs in the rest of the country did not understand their problems. Queen Mary's Lady-in-Waiting wrote to a friend,

> In 1931 I motored through the north of England. The drive was a terrible eye-opener. We passed through towns and villages dead and deserted except for knots of men out of work.

Men and women went on hunger marches to London to protest that their dole money was too little. People on the way saw what it was like to be out of work.

In Jarrow, near Newcastle-on-Tyne, almost everybody worked for the shipyard. In 1934 it closed and most Jarrow men lost their jobs. A writer said,

> Jarrow is derelict. One out of every two shops seemed to be permanently closed.

▲ The march from Jarrow to London was 450 kilometres. What are the men in the front doing?

▼ Jarrow marchers get their evening meal. The Boy Scouts helped the marchers by giving them cooking equipment.

In 1936 Ellen Wilkinson, Jarrow's MP, led 207 men on a hunger march. They had raised £800 to buy groundsheets to protect the men in rain and an old bus to carry blankets and kit. They bought leather and nails for the men to mend their boots. They saved £1 for each man's train fare home from London.

Doctors and medical students looked after the men's sore feet at night. Most people welcomed and fed the men. After a month, the men reached London to give the Prime Minister a petition (a list of signatures) asking for help. Sadly, little was done for Jarrow.

a Why were the early 1930s called the Depression? Is it a good name or can you think of a better one?

a Work out a route for the Jarrow Marchers to march to London calling in at as many of the major towns as possible.

b Make up a song or poem about the Jarrow March.

New Industries in the South

London shops full of luxuries like cameras, crisps, nylon stockings, vacuum cleaners, radios, toothpaste and scent amazed the Jarrow marchers. More people in the south had jobs than in the north, and those with jobs could afford to buy luxuries.

▶ Piccadilly Circus just before 1930. Rich people in evening clothes hurry to theatres and cinemas in London.

A boy remembered London as,

> A warm and colourful place with its red buses and trams, trees, advertising placards, the lights, the bright Underground stations... the shops looked inviting.

The shops sold goods made on electric machines in new factories. These '**new industries**' around London and the Midlands sold most of their products in this country. A writer described a Midlands city,

> Coventry...made bicycles when everybody was cycling, cars when everybody wanted a motor, and now it is busy with aeroplanes, wireless sets, and various electrical contrivances...There are still plenty of unemployed here... but Coventry should be all right.

Working women

Women in the new factories did delicate work like wiring radios. They earned less than men for the same job. A girl might be sacked when she reached 18, for at that age her wages were meant to go up.

▶ The Hoover factory was built in the 1930s near London. Do you know what was made here?

Many worked on a production line with long conveyor belts. They did the same small job, hour after hour. One woman remembered,

> My husband complained he might as well have a wooden wife. I'm that tired at the end of the evening I'm fit for nothing.

▼ Woolworths shop assistants. Many women worked in shops. It was more interesting than factory work but a woman might be standing on her feet ten hours a day.

Although most women had jobs in factories or offices, thousands still worked as domestic servants for rich people, just as they did in Victorian times. The work was very hard and the pay was very low. A writer described one woman's day,

> She works from 6.30 am till after 9 pm with one half-day off a week and alternative Sunday afternoons. She sleeps in a tiny bedroom which is very hot in summer and bitterly cold in winter.

Dream houses

▲ Hundreds of new 1930s houses had small gardens and garages. To buy this house would have cost you just under 50p a week.

People with well-paid jobs could afford to buy new houses. Hundreds were built in **suburbs** near the crowded cities. A house advert read,

> A palace in miniature only half-an-hour from London...amid the healthy atmosphere of Nature in her most beautiful aspects.

Electricity and new gadgets made housework easier. A gas water heater advert ran,

> Happy in the morning,
> As the water's hot,
> We can bath an army,
> The Ascot's done the lot.

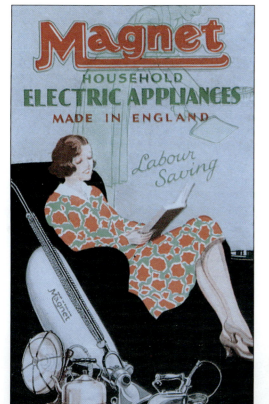

◄ An advert for early electrical household gadgets. Can you recognise what each one is used for?

- **a** What is a suburb? Why were they built?
- **a** Look at each main character in the painting on page 11 and write down three things about them (such as are they rich or poor, or what job do they do).
- **b** Compare and contrast the Woolworths shop on page 12 with a similar shop today.
- **a** With your teacher, choose a street or area nearby and do a survey of all the buildings built in the 1930s. How can you find out which they are?

Transport

Most people used public transport to travel in towns and cities. London's Underground trains carried thousands of people. Buses began to replace rattling old trams because they did not need lines to run on.

▶ Trams could only run where there were lines. How many other types of transport can you see in this picture?

Railways

In the 1930s Britain had four railway companies, the Southern, the London Midland & Scottish, the London & North Eastern and the Great Western. They had thousands more stations and miles of lines than today. Tiny villages had stations called 'halts.'

Most railways made more money from goods than passengers. There were long coal trains, milk trains, fish trains from ports and trains at harvest time. Slow mixed goods trains had lots of different waggons carrying anything from a horse to a car.

▼ A mixed goods train. British Rail no longer runs any trains like this.

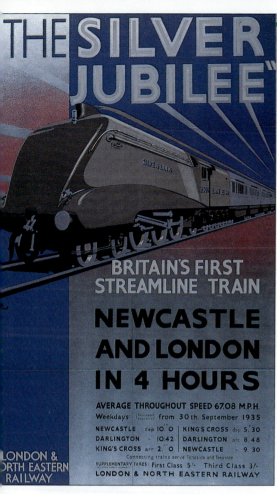

▲ This express train celebrated King George V's Silver Jubilee in 1935, when he had been king for 25 years.

They stopped at stations to pick up waggons or drop them off. Lorries took goods to and from stations.

People travelled long distances by express trains with sleeping cars and restaurant cars where waiters served tasty food from silver trays. One even had a cinema coach.

In 1935 a 'streamlined' express ran for the first time. A driver proudly remembered,

> She was the finest engine I ever rode on. I didn't know accurately what speed we were doing. I judged it to be about 90 miles an hour. Mr Gresley, who had designed the engine, shouted in my ear, "Ease your arm, young man! Do you know you've touched 112 [mph] twice!"

Roads

The railways lost business to the roads. New factories were built by new roads, and lorries delivered straight to shops. There were more cars, too. Fred Haigh (see page 2) was not rich, but he loved the freedom of driving and hated trains. He was a chauffeur at a Sheffield mine. He wore a uniform and drove the owners around in cars. Fred remembered,

> I had a licence in 1919, when I was 16. There were no driving tests then. There were very few cars on the road, and not many people could drive. If you could drive, you could usually get a job.

▶ Do you think this advert is for an expensive car or a cheap one? Why?

▼ A motorcycle combination. Not all roads were as bad as this one.

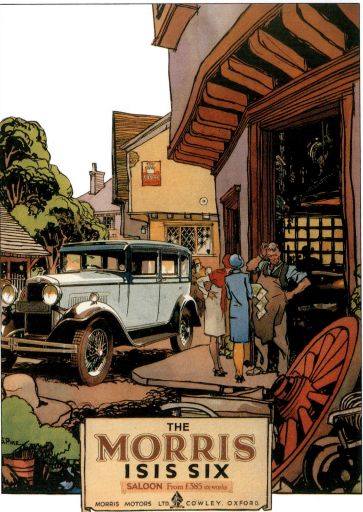

In 1935 a new Ford car cost £100. It was unheated and you defrosted the windscreen with a hot water bottle. A motorbike with a sidecar, called a 'motorcycle combination', was cheaper. One man complained,

> I'm out in the rain driving the motorbike, and I can see Betty and the kids eating sweets in the sidecar.

Driving was dangerous. In 1934 more people died on the roads than in 1980, when many more cars were on the roads. Traffic lights were first used in 1931, but roads did not become safer until driving tests and a 30 mph town speed limit began in 1935.

Ships and planes

Most people took about four days to cross the Atlantic to America. They went on great liners (ships) like floating hotels. Vast gas-filled airships were much faster, but some crashed, causing huge gas explosions. There were no jets, and propellor planes could not go far without stopping. An air hostess remembered refuelling a plane,

> Some of us had to join bucket brigades to help fuel the planes. If the weather got bad we would land in a field for a while and wait for the storm to clear up.

▼ The *Queen Mary* was the world's biggest passenger ship when she was built in 1936 in Glasgow.

▶ The dining room of the *Queen Mary* was as luxurious as the best hotels.

◐ **a** Have a class debate about the advantages and disadvantages of road transport in the 1930s.

◩ **a** Design a 1930s poster advertising journeys across the Atlantic in a large liner. Use the information in this chapter.

△ **a** Prepare a short talk called "Land, Sea and Air" about travel in the 1930s, using information from this chapter and from other books.

Fun and Holidays

▶ Comics were even more popular in the 1930s than today. This is the first *Dandy*, from 1937.

▼ A gas street lamp had more uses than just lighting a street!

Some lucky children had dolls houses and train sets to play with. Near London, they might have seen the first television broadcasts in 1936. But children usually made up their own games. Two adults remembered,

> We played out in the street all the time...marbles, hoops, hopscotch. When it started to get dark early you could get away with all sorts of mischief.

> Every lamp post had a wicket chalked to it. On summer evenings it was the rope skipping season.

Radio and dancing

Most people listened to the radio. Families sat in silence to enjoy radio plays. Young and old, rich and poor enjoyed Henry Hall's big band and other radio stars. Local bands in hundreds of dance halls copied the radio stars. Girls often went dancing at the *Palais* or *Mecca* several times a week. They could learn new dances like the foxtrot at dance schools.

Cinema

People loved the cinema, especially after 'talkies' began replacing silent films in 1930. There were lots of cinemas. Bolton, for example, had 28. Now it has just one. Two people remembered the pictures,

> The pictures help you live in another world for a little while. I almost feel I'm in the picture.

> Everybody went on a Saturday night. It was a lovely little pictures. It had a balcony and we really enjoyed going. Best of all we loved the organ. It rose slowly in front of the screen, the organist played a tune with twiddly bits, then waved his hand and the organ sank into the ground!

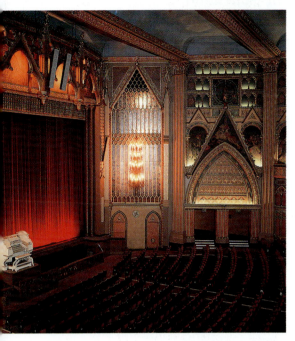

▲ A large cinema with an organ. It opened in 1931. Is your local cinema as decorative as this one?

▶ Many 1930s cinemas have now been pulled down or turned into bingo halls like this one. Some larger ones are divided into three or four 'mini' cinemas.

Holidays

Most holiday-makers went to seaside towns like Skegness or Southend and stayed in boarding houses. A woman remembered a friendly landlady in Blackpool, where Fred and Jessie Haigh had their honeymoon,

> Each day we would go and buy our own meat or fish for the day and Mrs Cavanagh did all the cooking. We went 13 years running, it was like home from home.

Only the rich took holidays abroad. Most people would have agreed with a Londoner who said,

> We never thought of going to places like Spain or Portugal. The only time we heard about such places was when a war was on.

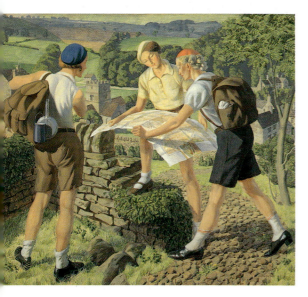

▲ Hiking in the countryside was cheap and popular in the 1930s. Why do you think city people enjoyed it so much?

- **a** Make a list of words and phrases describing the cinema in the 1930s. Make a similar list for the 1990s. Underline those words which appear on both lists.

- **b** Design an advertisement for a train ride to the seaside. Make sure that you get your facts right.

- **a** Look at a current TV guide. Can you find films made in the 1930s?

The Second World War

▲ Adolf Hitler salutes troops from his car.

The Depression was worse in Germany than Britain. In 1933 Adolf Hitler became Germany's leader. He said he would make Germany great again and give Germans jobs. He **rearmed** the airforce, navy and army, which helped make factories busy again.

Hitler threatened nearby countries which he said were part of Germany. In March 1939 Britain promised to help Poland if Hitler attacked. Britain began rearming. The old industries grew busy again and many British workers had their first jobs in years.

On 1 September 1939 Germany invaded Poland. Two days later, Prime Minister Neville Chamberlain spoke on the radio to say Britain was at war with Germany. The war spread across the world and countries took sides. Britain and the **British Empire**, together with the USA and Russia, fought against Germany, Italy and Japan.

Gas masks

Poison gas killed thousands of soldiers in the First World War. In 1939 Britons feared Germany would bomb them with gas. It did not happen, but everyone carried a gas mask in a cardboard box just in case.

▶ Gas masks were uncomfortable and the glasses soon steamed up. After the war, children used them as toys.

Evacuation

▶ Children about to be evacuated in 1940. What are the children carrying in their cardboard boxes?

▼ This greetings card was printed for evacuated children. Design your own greetings card to send to an evacuee.

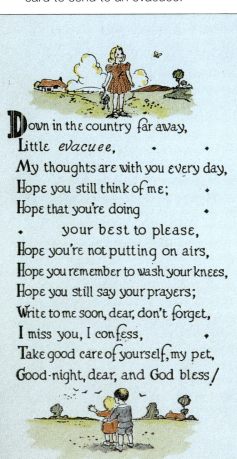

Down in the country far away,
Little evacuee,
My thoughts are with you every day,
Hope you still think of me;
Hope that you're doing
your best to please,
Hope you're not putting on airs,
Hope you remember to wash your knees,
Hope you still say your prayers;
Write to me soon, dear, don't forget,
I miss you, I confess,
Take good care of yourself, my pet,
Good-night, dear, and God bless!

When war began, the government **evacuated**, or sent away, city children to the country, safe from the danger of German bombs. Evacuees older than five went with their teachers, leaving their parents behind. Two girls remembered,

We left home early in the morning with our gas masks hanging round our necks. We got to school and all the mothers looked very grim. They were trying not to cry. We didn't cry because we didn't know what was happening to us.

I got off at a station in Devon. They took us to a church hall and grown-ups came in and said, "I'll take those two", "She looks nice, she'll do". Then there was just me and another boy left.

Many children loved their new families and made friendships for life. Some had never seen the country before. A boy wrote home,

They call this spring, Mum, and they have one down here every year.

▲ Government posters tried to persuade mothers not to let their children return from the country to the cities. Who is the ghostly figure standing up?

Other children were miserable. Some even ran away to get back home. This is what one girl remembered,

> The children shouted out at me, "Go back to London, we don't want you here". They held me down and put snails and frogs in my dress.

Poor children shocked country people. A woman wrote,

> One boy had never had a bath before; his ribs looked black... Some children had never used a knife and fork.

Poor children could hardly believe what they saw in their new homes. A 13-year-old child wrote home,

> Everything was so clean. We were given flannels and toothbrushes. We'd never cleaned our teeth up till then. And hot water came from the tap. And there was a lavatory upstairs. And carpets.

- **a** Discuss whether evacuation was a good or bad idea. Use the evidence in this chapter.
- **a** Imagine you are one of the children in the photo on page 22. Write a letter home explaining how you feel as an evacuee.
- **b** Design a poster to show parents how dangerous it was to leave their children in the cities during the war.

Off to War

Thousands of young men joked or sang as they left to fight the Germans in France. A few months later, in 1940, the Germans trapped the British on a beach at Dunkirk. A huge fleet of boats, from holiday ferries to tiny motor boats, set sail from Britain to rescue the men from France.

▶ British soldiers leaving for France in 1939.

Britain stood alone against the German blitzkrieg ('lightning war') that had overrun Europe. German planes, warships, and soldiers in Norway, Holland, Belgium and France threatened Britain. Hitler planned to invade Britain in September 1940.

Britons were scared. The new Prime Minister, Winston Churchill, spoke on the radio to encourage them,

▼ Winston Churchill made radio speeches to encourage people when they thought Britain would lose the war.

> We shall fight on the beaches, we shall fight on the landing grounds, we shall fight in the fields and in the streets, we shall fight in the hills; we shall never surrender.

Road signs and station names were removed or painted out to confuse invaders. It confused British people, too, and many got off at the wrong stations!

Older men joined the Home Guard to protect Britain from invaders. They often had only pitchforks or old rifles to fight off the Germans.

◀ People joked about the Home Guard. This photograph is from a 1970s TV comedy series called *Dad's Army*.

The Battle of Britain

Before Hitler could invade Britain, he had to defeat the Royal Air Force so that it could not attack his invasion troops. Germany's **Luftwaffe** had more pilots and fighter planes than the RAF. In 1940 British and German pilots fought the Battle of Britain mostly over southern England. In the confusion, RAF Spitfire and Hurricane fighter plane pilots thought that they had shot down more German planes than they really had.

A radio reporter described a battle 'live',

> Somebody's hit a German – and he's coming down – there's a long streak of smoke – ah, the man's baled out by parachute – he's a Junkers 87 and he's going slap into the sea and there he goes – sma-a-sh...Oh boy, I've never seen anything so good as this – the RAF boys have really got these boys taped.

▲ German and British fighter planes in the Battle of Britain. They twisted and dived in 'dog fights' and left white vapour trails behind them.

A fighter pilot described it rather differently,

> It was no picnic despite what anyone might say... Most of us were pretty scared all the time; you only felt happy when the battle was over and you were on your way home, then you were safe for a bit.

Germany failed to defeat the RAF. The Luftwaffe had lost too many pilots and planes. In autumn 1940 Hitler gave up his invasion plans. The Battle of Britain had been won. Churchill said,

> Never in the field of human conflict was so much owed by so many to so few.

a Do you think it is a good idea to make TV comedies about the war, such as *Dad's Army* and *'Allo, 'Allo*?

a Why did the Germans try to drive the RAF from the sky?

b If a pilot returned from battle and said that he had shot down one of the enemy, how could you check whether his story was true?

c Choose three words to describe the radio reporter's description of the Battle of Britain and three words for the pilot's description. Discuss the difference between them both.

d Look at the painting of the Battle of Britain on page 26. Do you think this is reliable or unreliable evidence about the battle?

a Find out about the planes that fought each other in the Battle of Britain. What were their names and what did they look like?

The Blitz

After the Battle of Britain, German planes turned to bombing cities. This was called the **blitz**, short for blitzkrieg. Germany tried to destroy railways and weapons factories. They also bombed people to try and make them give up. During the worst months, in 1940 and 1941, 45,000 people were killed by German bombs. Nearly half lived in London, the worst-hit city.

Fire watchers looked out for fire bombs that set buildings alight. They tried to put them out with sand buckets. 'HE' (high explosive) bombs destroyed buildings and killed people and could land anywhere. Two people remembered the terrible damage they did,

> In the middle of the street lay the remains of a baby. It had been blown clean through the window... I found a torn piece of curtain in which to wrap it.

> Broken glass everywhere, half the garden scorched by incendiary bombs, and two houses nothing but a pile of rubble.

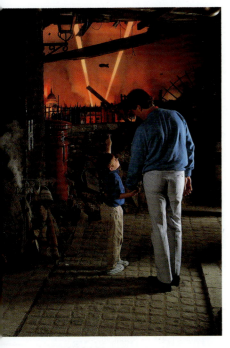

▲ This is a modern museum exhibit of the London blitz.

▶ Liverpool's city centre in the blitz. The city was one of Britain's biggest ports and was bombed many times.

The black out and sirens

German bombers flew at night. Darkness was the best defence against British guns. People blacked out lights to stop bombers aiming on them. Car drivers dimmed their headlamps until they could hardly see. There were many more road accidents.

▶ The game on the right shows children fixing a black-out curtain. Next to it is a government leaflet. Why did the umbrella on the card have a bold black and white pattern?

▲ Air raid wardens cleared up after raids and helped rescue people.

When German bombers were coming, sirens on roofs wailed a frightening warning. People who lived in the war never forgot the sound. Jessie Haigh says,

> I used to start shaking when the siren went. I couldn't stop. We didn't go out to the shelter much, but I had an armchair in the cubby hole under the stairs and we used to sit in there.

Shelters

Before the war, the government gave away millions of Anderson shelters. Six people could shelter in the corrugated steel sunk into a garden. Today some are used as garden sheds. The shelter was no use if you were away from home, and many people had no gardens.

▶ A mother reads to her children inside an Anderson shelter.

Public shelters were built to hold hundreds of people. Jessie Haigh remembers her niece going to the theatre one night in Sheffield,

▲ Shelterers on the Underground liked having company and often sang songs together.

> When the bombing started, she and the others were led outside to the shelters. She and her friend spent the night in the shelter. Next day she took her friend home, but the whole street was in ruins. Her friend collapsed because she thought her family had been killed, but luckily they were all safe in a shelter.

Later in the war, Londoners began sheltering in stations deep in the Underground railways. A man remembered his childhood in the shelters,

> I got bars and bars of chocolate out of machines and weighed myself incessantly. Here was a new life, a whole city under the world. We rode up and down the escalators and I used to ride in the trains to see the other stations of underground people.

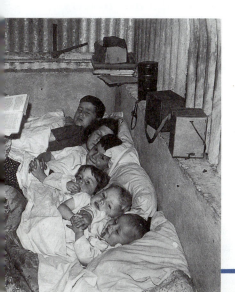

a On a map of your street make plans for the placing of a public shelter in case of air attack. List the five most important things that you think should be taken with you into the shelter.

b Imagine you are living in a city during the blitz. Write to your cousin in the country describing the dangers. Remember the dangers of the black out as well as the bombing.

a Anderson shelters were made from corrugated metal. Test the strength of corrugated material compared with non-corrugated material of the same type (use card). Record your results.

Rationing and the War Effort

Food was short because German submarines sank many ships bringing food to Britain from America. Some food vanished from the shops. You needed a doctor's note to get oranges.

Food had to be shared out carefully. This was called **rationing**. Even King George VI had a ration book. Shopkeepers cut out 'coupons' from your book if you bought rationed food. When the coupons ran out you could not buy any more. You had to use the same shops all the time and your shopkeeper kept your name in a register.

Fred and Jessie Haigh often got more food than their ration because they lived in the country. People kept pigs or chickens and killed them for meat. Eggs were rare in cities. A Dorset woman had a London friend to stay who

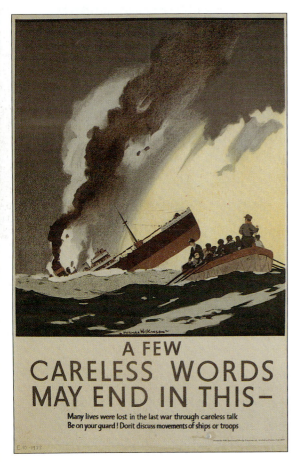

▲ How could 'careless talk' lead to this ship being sunk by German submarines?

...had not had an egg for six months and was delighted because we had two each for tea.

If harvests were bad or submarines sunk more ships bringing food from the USA, rations were cut. Milk and eggs are mostly water. To save cargo space, dried milk and egg were imported. The egg powder made rubbery omlettes when it was cooked.

◄ This was one adult's supply of rationed food for one week.

▲ The government encouraged everybody to grow vegetables to help out with the rations.

American tinned corned beef and Spam helped out with fresh meat rations. People used all sorts of things to replace food that vanished. Nettles tasted like spinach when boiled and could be dried for tea. Sugar and sweets were rare. It was illegal to ice cakes, so people hired cardboard wedding cakes for show. Women made jam and cakes with carrots.

▶ People dug up gardens and even parks to plant vegetables.

Salvage

▼ The government urged people to save everything. You had different dustbins for paper, pig swill (waste food for pigs), tins, rags, bones and glass.

Nothing was wasted in the effort to win the war. You saved waste paper and scrap metal as 'salvage' (we call it 'recycling' today). Newspapers encouraged people to hand in aluminium pots and pans, saying,

> We will turn your pots and pans into Spitfires and Hurricanes.

However, few were ever turned into planes.

Women melted down old lipstick ends to make new ones and made up their eyes with soot. They painted gravy browning and pencilled seams on their legs to look like nylon stockings, which were very hard to get.

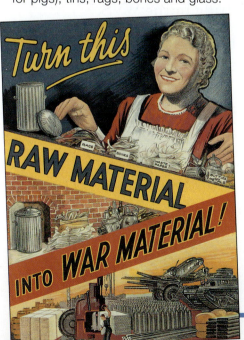

War work

Everybody did their bit to help the war effort. Most men who were not too old joined the army, navy or airforce. Many women joined the services, too, but they did not fight. Other women did men's jobs.

▲ The Women's Land Army helped with farm work such as harvesting. Colour photographs were rare in the 1940s.

▲ Women did men's work in the war. Some drove buses or worked on the railways.

People did all sorts of unpaid voluntary work. The Women's Voluntary Service (WVS) ran soldiers' tea bars. Jessie Haigh joined the WVS and gave out ration cards. She rolled up bandages for the injured and made camouflage netting in the WVS.

Sheffield was badly bombed. Fred Haigh often saw bombers overhead. He kept his old job but after work he was a 'Special Constable', a part-time policeman. At night he made sure people kept the black out. If he saw a light, he shouted, "Put that light out!" One night he went out to guard an unexploded bomb,

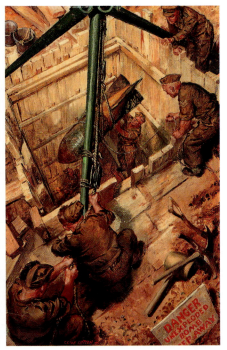

▲ Soldiers gently hoist up a buried unexploded bomb.

> We sat there for ages, hoping it would go off so we could go home. When it did go off, it blew us all off the wall we were sitting on and covered us with mud!

A woman remembered knitting for men in the forces,

> We collected wool pennies each week. Then we bought wool and made balaclava helmets and gloves as well as socks and seaboot stockings.

However, one boy, whose father was a sailor, said,

> My father, when returning from a voyage, would bring home sweaters, scarves, gloves, balaclava helmets and suchlike knitted by patriotic ladies. We could wear a different colour balaclava every day.

▲ The RAF book of knitting patterns.

a Have a class debate about rationing. Each side needs to say why they think that it is fair or unfair.

a Draw a quick sketch of a wedding in 1942. Write notes around the sketch to show how rationing had affected the wedding (for example, the bride used melted down scraps of lipstick, and so on).

b Prepare a two-minute radio broadcast to explain to people how they can help the war effort. Do a presentation to the class.

c Write a job description for the following: Special Constable, a member of the WVS, an air raid warden.

Relaxing

People visited theatres or cinemas to forget the war. Even more people went to the cinema than before the war. Drinkers stood around pub pianos and sang loudly to drown the noise of the bombs outside.

▶ A popular comedy film made fun of Hitler and the Germans. What is the sign on the goose's neck?

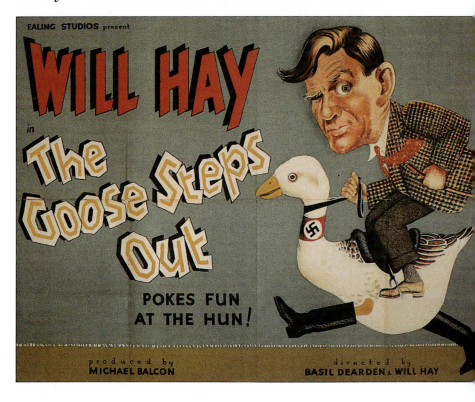

Radio

Radio was vital. People listened in a hush to news. There were two radio channels, the 'Home Service', with news of the war and serious programmes, and the 'Forces Programme', with popular music and comedy shows.

Tommy Handley's 'ITMA' stood for 'It's That Man Again'. Thirty million people listened to it. You had to listen carefully to get all the quick jokes. 'TTFN' (Ta-ta For Now) was an ITMA catchword all over Britain, and ITMA always ended with an abbreviation like 'NKABTYSIRWU' (Never Kiss A Baby Till You're Sure It's Right Way Up).

◀ Radio stars on the cover of a comic annual.

Music and dancing

Factories worked non-stop on war production. There were day shifts and night shifts. Entertaining the workers was important. A saxophone player who worked in a Coventry plane factory said,

> My foreman on nights was desperately keen to get some sort of show going for the night shift. There was total blackout, enemy aircraft were passing overhead most nights. Public transport finished early and the pubs closed at 9pm. Petrol was rationed. However, Les persuaded a few of the band who lived in the area to come in and do a show.

Soldiers loved dancing. Gerald Haigh's uncle was a drummer in the 'Embassy Dance Band', and his uncle's brother played piano. Gerald spent many happy hours on the stage, listening to and watching the band.

▶ A dance band in 1944. ATS stood for 'Auxiliary Territorial Service', a special part of the army for women.

- **a** Discuss the importance of radio during the war. Use the evidence of radio in the war section of this book.

- **a** Can you make up an amusing abbreviation for the ITMA programme? Listen to a tape of an ITMA programme if you can.

- **b** *Music While you Work* was a radio programme designed to keep the workers happily working. Find out what songs and music were popular during the war.

The End of the War

The USA joined the war on Britain's side in 1941. American soldiers called 'General Infantrymen' came to Britain in 1943. Everyone called them 'GIs'. Children loved them and a boy fondly remembered,

> We had a camp in our town. We'd hang around to ask for gum and sweets. One black GI was fat. He'd pat our heads and with a wink and smile let us in to see their films.

The GIs left with a huge army of troops from Britain and other countries to invade Europe and defeat Germany. The **Allied troops** landed in France on 6 June 1944, which was called 'D' Day.

American and British planes bombed German cities until few buildings were left standing. On the ground the Allied troops fought bitter battles against the Germans. Russian troops forced German troops out of Eastern Europe. At last, on 7 May 1945, Germany surrendered.

Church bells were silent in the war. They were only to be rung if Britain was invaded. When peace came, every church bell rang out. Ships' hooters sounded in victory. People danced for joy in the streets.

▲ Black GIs at a night club. Many British people had never seen black people before the war.

▶ Manchester people celebrate the end of the war with Germany.

Children all over Britain had street parties and special food that had been a rare treat in the war. A girl wrote,

> Our street had a great big party and everyone painted their houses, red, white and blue. We had nice things to eat, even a cake. My Aunty Al got her piano out and played in the street, and everyone was dancing and singing. In school next day we all got an apple from Canada. It was beautiful, big and red.

▶ A children's victory celebration party.

The war in the East against Japan lasted until 14 August 1945. Japan only surrendered after the USA dropped two atomic bombs on the cities of Nagasaki and Hiroshima, causing great destruction.

a Study the photo on page 37. Write an article for the local paper on the victory party.

Britain after the War

Shortages

After the war, cities, factories, railways and houses lay in ruins. It was time to rebuild but everything was in short supply. A woman said,

> It was queues for everything, even if you didn't know what you were queuing for... you joined it because you knew there was something at the end of it.

▶ Queuing for coal sold off the back of a lorry.

In 1948 food rations were even smaller than during the war. People ate whale meat and a revolting fish called snoek because they were not rationed.

Bread was rationed for the first time in 1946. Bread Units, or 'BUs', allowed adults two loaves a week. A child under six had one loaf. If you had bread with soup in a restaurant, you could not have pudding.

Clothing coupons came with food ration books. A warning on the cover read,

> Detach this book at once and keep it safely. It is your only means of buying clothes.

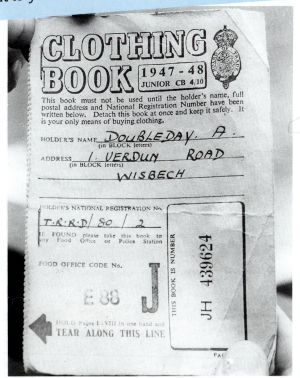

▶ A clothes ration book.

Food rationing only ended when meat came off ration in 1954. Gerald remembers sweets coming off in 1953,

> Suddenly, in the school tuckshop, we could buy whatever we wanted. It didn't seem real somehow. For as long as I could remember I never had a whole Mars bar. My mother had always cut them up neatly with the bread knife, for us to share.

Winter 1947

January 1947 was the coldest winter since 1894. Passenger trains were stuck in snow drifts for over a day. To save coal, you could not use electricity at home for five hours a day. Three million factory workers had to stop work when the power stations ran out of coal. It seemed worse than the war.

A Better Britain for All

A woman explained how people felt after the war,

> We expected at first a lot was going to be different, a lot was going to be better... A lot of us were disappointed.

Everyone wanted things to be better after all the suffering. They planned an end to poverty. They wanted the government to pay all unemployed people and old-age pensioners enough to live decent lives. They wanted free health care, better schools and houses and a government which made sure everybody had a job. Parliament made laws to try and do all these things.

▶ This wartime poster looked forward to the end of the war and peace, when Britain would have better hospitals and health care.

The National Health Service

In the 1930s people could buy insurance stamps from companies to pay for visits to the doctor. Poor people without stamps might be allowed to pay doctors what they could afford. A woman remembered,

> We never had a doctor because he charged 3/6 [18p] a visit and had to be paid on the dot.

A woman who had a baby just before midnight on 4 July 1948 paid her doctor £6. It would have been free after midnight when the National Health Service was introduced. Medicine, operations, doctors' visits, spectacles, even wigs were free on the NHS.

Gerald Haigh's friend had a bad limp caused by an illness called 'polio'. Few people died of polio, but if you caught it you might wake up to find a leg or arm did not work. In the 1950s, a **vaccine** was developed to stop polio. All children had free NHS vaccinations. Today polio is unknown in Britain.

▲ Why are these people here?

Housing

A big problem after the war was finding somewhere to live. There were not enough houses. People called 'squatters' took over empty buildings without permission. Some were turned out, but they were often left alone. They had nowhere else to go.

New houses take months to build and bricks and wood were hard to get. So the government built 125,000 prefabricated two-bedroom bungalows in factories. The 'prefabs' were bolted together on site and were built to last ten years. A few are still used today.

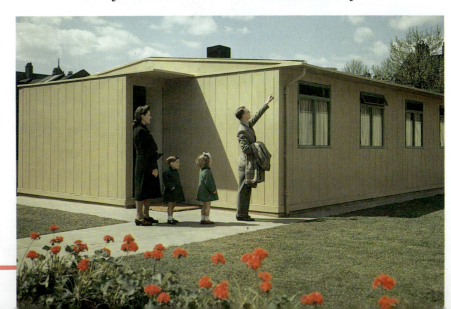

▶ A family looks at a new prefab. Many prefabs were made in the factories that once made bombers.

New Towns

In 1946 the government planned to build 14 new towns. Nye Bevan, Minister of Health, explained,

> I hope old people will not live in colonies of their own – they do not want to look out of their windows on endless processions of funerals of their friends... We should introduce into our modern towns the lovely feature of English and Welsh villages, where the doctor, the grocer, the butcher and the farm labourer all lived in the same street.

A woman remembered her new house in Hemel Hempstead,

> When I went upstairs to explore there was one bedroom, and another bedroom, a bathroom and an airing cupboard and another room down the end... I went and had a look, and I had three bedrooms which made me come downstairs, sit on the bottom step and howl. I wept because I was so happy.

▲ A map of the new towns. Where were most of them built?

▼ A sitting room furnished in the styles of the 1950s.

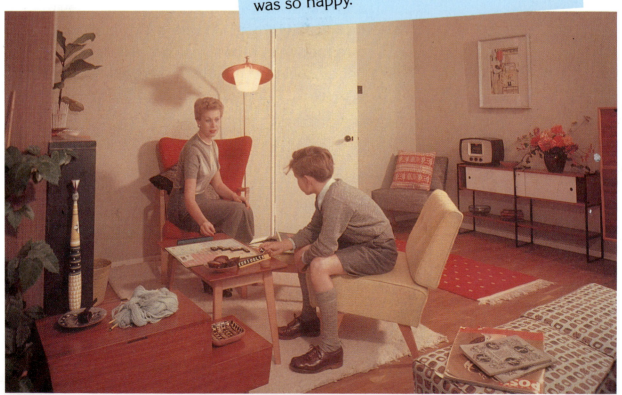

Muck and Smoke

Most houses in the cities still had coal fires. Factories and railway engines poured out clouds of thick black smoke. A woman said,

> If the wind blew from the mills, my clothes on the line got covered in black grit before they dried. I'd have to wash them again. God knows what it did to my lungs.

Smoke and fog mixed to make thick winter 'smogs'. Choking smog made people with bad chests ill and killed thousands of old people. In 1956 the Clean Air Act made people burn smokeless fuel.

The Festival of Britain

The 1851 Great Exhibition in London showed off British achievements and inventions. In 1951 the government decided to remember the Great Exhibition with a new Festival of Britain to cheer up people after the war and all the shortages. London held the main exhibition. As well as all the exhibits, there was a zoo and a funny train for visitors to ride.

▲ The logo (official sign) of the Festival of Britain.

▶ One of the Far Tottering and Oyster Creek Railway engines at the Festival of Britain. A sign on the railway read, "Do NOT tease the engines."

▲ The Festival of Britain at night. It was built on a bomb site on the side of the River Thames. All that remains today is the Royal Festival Hall, the big building with a rounded roof in the centre.

Gerald Haigh remembers the Festival well. He went there on a school trip.

> We camped at Slough, and went in to London on the train every day. The exhibition was wonderful – architecture straight out of science fiction. There were modern cars and railway engines on show, and all sorts of other inventions.

a You are writing a dictionary. Write down the entries for smog, New Towns, the Festival of Britain and prefabs.

b Draw three items from the photo of a living room on page 42 and draw the same items from your own living room. List the similarities and differences.

c Design a souvenir for the Festival of Britain showing the logo.

You've Never Had It So Good

In 1957 the Prime Minister, Harold Macmillan said,

> Most of our people have never had it so good.

He was right. In the 1950s factories exported things all over the world. Most people had jobs and had more money to spend than anyone could remember.

People could afford the new goods advertised in magazines. Electrical appliances saved women from hard work.

The coronation

King George VI died in 1952. People were excited when his daughter was crowned Queen Elizabeth II in 1953. Her coronation seemed to show that the hard times after the war were really over. People talked of a new Elizabethan Age, like the age of Elizabeth I. New discoveries seemed to happen every day. Here are a few events from 1952 and 1953.

Britain's Comet flew. It was the world's first jet airliner. Mount Everest was climbed for the first time. John Cobb set a water-speed record in Scotland at 330 kph. Britain exploded her first atomic bomb. ICI began making 'Terylene', an artificial cloth.

▲ Just before the coronation, Britons read in their newspapers that Mount Everest had been climbed for the first time.

▶ Thousands of people lined London's streets to watch the queen's coronation coach pass.

Television

The BBC televised the coronation and 20 million people watched it. It was the first time more people saw a big event on television than heard it on radio. One man who saw it as a young boy said,

> It was a cold, wet day and we huddled in blankets round a set grandad hired. Gran served sandwiches as we watched the tiny, flickering grey screen. I thought she'd invited in half the street to watch.

Television was so popular that people went out less and less to enjoy themselves. Many cinemas closed. In 1955 ITV began. It had catchy adverts that children sang like pop tunes.

▲ Children loved TV right from the start. Parents often only let them watch Children's Hour.

▶ One of the first TV adverts for PG Tips tea.

▶ The graph on the left shows how television became more and more popular. The graph on the right shows how fewer and fewer people went to the cinema in the same years. Do you think there is a connection?

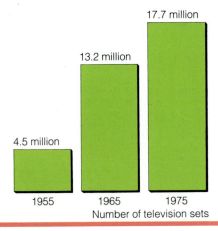

Number of television sets

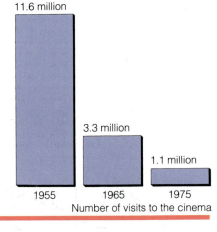

Number of visits to the cinema

Teenagers

Young people in the 1950s did not want to be like their parents. They had enough money to dress differently and enjoy their own music. They even had a new name - teenagers. A boy said in 1957,

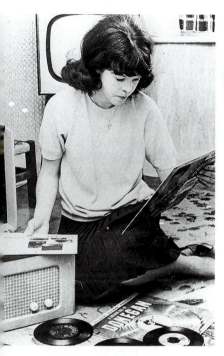

▲ A teenager listens to records on an 'autochanger' record player.

▼ Two teenagers 'jiving'.

I got my first job as a clerk in a steel works. There was no shortage of jobs. I stood in a phone box one afternoon and every firm I rang up had vacancies.

I earned £10 a week. My father, who had been working like a slave for 30 years, was earning £7 10s [£7.50]. I lived at home and gave my mother a couple of pounds for food. The rest was mine.

I bought a scooter to go around on, and a good record player. Every Saturday I bought a new long-playing record. I went to the best men's hairdresser in town every fortnight. I went to the pictures with a crowd twice a week. On Sunday nights we went to the pub.

A favourite place to meet was the coffee bar. A London man laughed as he remembered,

We'd sit all night at *Gino*'s. A huge shiny espresso coffee machine hissed steam. The place was lit by candles in bottles and the red glow of a jukebox. I think the gloom kept older people out. We liked to look tough, but all we did was listen to records and talk about girls and clothes.

▲ The latest fashions at a hairdressers. Teddy boys plastered cream into their hair and carefully combed it into shape in front of a mirror.

Young people and parents wore the same fashions in the 1930s. Teenagers in the 1950s had their own styles to show they were different.

One style was the 'teddy boy' look. Teddy boys wore shoes with thick rubber soles, 'shocking' green or pink socks, tight 'drainpipe' trousers and long jackets with velvet collars. Teddy girls had ponytails that hung down over tight sweaters. Their skirts and starched petticoats flared out as they danced. A wide leather belt completed the look.

Rock and Roll

In 1956 an American film called *Rock around the Clock* came to Britain. It starred Bill Haley and his Comets. Teenagers went mad - jiving in cinemas and sometimes wrecking seats.

▶ Bill Haley playing guitar with the Comets.

Other American bands and singers, especially Elvis Presley, made British teenagers want to make their own music. You could buy a guitar for £7 or make a bass from a tea chest with string tied to a broom stick. Popular British singers like Cliff Richard, Lonnie Donegan and Tommy Steele copied the Americans.

New peoples

During the war, thousands of Europeans escaped to Britain. After the war, many stayed here. One man remembered a Polish man who lived in his street,

> My parents seemed to sense when he was walking down the road, and one of them would get up and look through the lace curtains. "There goes the Pole, mother," father would say. He was always called the Pole partly because we couldn't pronounce his real name, partly because he was not English.

In the 1950s, our factories and railways were so busy that they needed more workers. Many people in the Caribbean islands like Jamaica and Barbados had no work. Our hospitals, railways, bus companies and hotels persuaded them to come to live and work in Britain.

▶ Caribbean immigrants arrive by ship in Southampton.

Most people who **immigrated** to Britain came from the countries Britain once ruled, which were called the British Empire. When the countries began to rule themselves, the Empire became known as the **British Commonwealth** in 1947. The immigrants stood out because of their colour. Some people welcomed them and said they made Britain more interesting because they brought new foods and customs. Others did not like them, especially when there were fewer jobs in the 1960s. Some landlords would not rent houses to Indians or Caribbeans. Today this is illegal.

Commonwealth people came here to find a better life. Other Commonwealth countries invited skilled workers to **emigrate** from Britain and start better lives in Australia, South Africa, Canada and New Zealand.

   a Make a frieze of the coronation procession with the queen in the state coach.

   b List all the electrical appliances in the advert on page 45. List the same appliances in your home. What differences and similarities are there?

   c Design and label a cardboard cut-out of a teddy boy and girl.

   a Find out which countries immigrants to Britain came from after the Second World War. On an outline map of the world, draw arrows to Britain from these places.

   b Find out from grown-ups the pop stars and bands that played in the 1950s. Do you hear any of their music now?

Railways and Travel

The railways needed new trains and a lot of repairs after the war. In 1948 the government took them over. It said it could run them better than their owners. The four companies became one big company called British Railways, or BR. It was now a **nationalised** company owned by the British nation.

▶ Waterloo station, in London, just before nationalisation in 1948. The engines are painted in the green of the Southern Railway.

▲ The last steam engine ran on British Railways in 1968. Some people were very sad to see them go. Today people have rebuilt some of the old engines. They run railways as they were in the old days.

At first the plan worked and BR carried more goods with fewer engines, trucks and workers. New diesels began to replace steam engines. But by 1956 it was costing more to run the railways than they earned from passengers and goods. BR was losing money.

In 1963 the head of BR, Dr Beeching, saw that most of BR was hardly used. It had over 7000 stations, but made half its money from 118 big stations. He tried to save money by closing 2000 stations and 14,000 kilometres of lines. He tried to close more, but country people protested so much that some lines and stations were saved from the 'Beeching Axe'.

51

Cars

There were few cars after the war. Everyone wanted one, but tank and plane factories had only just begun making cars again. People paid huge sums for second-hand cars. If you were lucky and got a new car, you could sell it for much more than it cost.

Our factories exported more cars and motorbikes than any other country at the start of the 1950s. British shops had few cars to sell because most were sold abroad. Gerald Haigh's uncle ordered a Ford car at a Motor Show and had to wait six years to get one.

More people could afford cars, so fewer used trains. Many drove just at weekends or on holiday. Others drove to work in cities so they could live in the country. The new cars clogged up the narrow, winding roads, causing traffic jams. Something had to be done. The first long motorway, the M1, opened in 1958. More have been built since. More goods now go by road than by rail.

▲ The Motor Show in the 1950s.

▼ The first 'Mini' car was made in 1959. It became very fashionable and is still made today.

▶ The new M1 on a book cover.

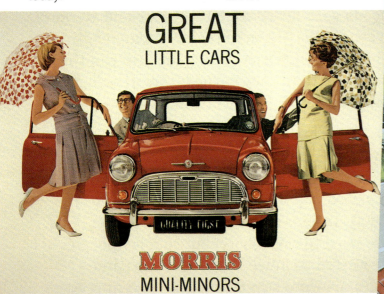

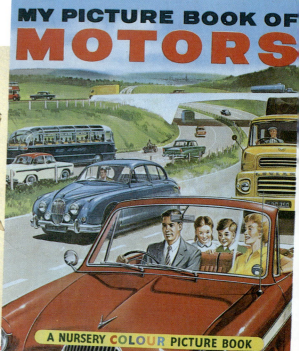

Planes and Ships

People still went to America in great passenger ships at the start of the 1950s. It still took four days to cross the Atlantic as before the war. By 1960, however, people flew to America in a few hours. Flying became less expensive, and by the 1960s ordinary people could afford to fly to Europe for holidays.

▶ Passengers leaving an airliner.

a Look at the painting of Waterloo Station on page 51. Imagine walking through the station and describe the people that you pass. What differences are there between this station and one now?

b Look at the picture of a motorway on page 52. List the differences between motoring then and now.

c Design a poster to persuade people that an old railway line ought to be brought back into use.

⚠ **a** Study an Ordnance Survey map of your area. See if you can find any railway lines or stations that are no longer in use. Can you find out what happened to them?

The 1960s

In the 1960s the whole world listened to British bands like the Beatles or Rolling Stones. The latest clothes and music came from London. A writer said,

> London was the hub of the world. Everybody was coming to London, the Americans, everyone, because that's where it was at.

Our factories did not do so well. More and more British people bought foreign cars or motorbikes. Gerald Haigh bought a German VW car in 1967. Japan began making transistor radios in the 1950s. Today you may play a Japanese computer game.

▲ The Beatles playing on a TV pop show.

▶ These are some Japanese goods from the 1960s.

▼ Older people in the 1960s often complained that young men dressed like women. Do you agree?

After 1945 men took back the jobs women had done in the war. It was only from the 1960s that women began to do 'men's work' in peacetime, such as bus driving or running firms. A 1970 law made employers pay women the same as men for the same work.

The Haigh family lived through the events described in this book. This is modern history. It is not like other history because we have memories to help us understand it. Ask grown-ups you know what happened to them during the events described in this book.

Glossary

allied troops	Troops from different countries who fought against Germany.
blitz	Hitler's bombing of British cities. It is short for blitzkrieg, which is German for 'lightning war'.
British Commonwealth	Most countries in the British Empire became part of the British Commonwealth when they began to rule themselves.
British Empire	A large group of countries once ruled by Britain.
Depression, the	The time in the 1930s when countries traded less and factories across the world closed down. Millions of people were unemployed.
dole	Money the government paid unemployed people in the 1930s.
emigrate	To leave your own country to live permanently in another.
evacuate	To move people away from one place to another.
export	To sell goods made in one country to another country.
immigrate	To move into and settle permanently in a new country.
import	To buy goods abroad and bring them into your own country.
Luftwaffe	The German air force.
nationalise	A government nationalises a private company when it takes it over to own and run it for the nation, or people of a country.
new industries	New industries in the 1930s made modern goods, such as radios, cars, cameras or light bulbs, in factories with modern machines.
old industries	Industries like cotton spinning and weaving that began in Victorian times or earlier. Most used old-fashioned machinery.
rations	Shares of something that is in short supply.
rearm	To enlarge the army, navy and airforce with new weapons.
suburbs	Groups of houses built just outside a city or large town.
trade	When countries buy from and sell to each other.
vaccine	Doctors give vaccines to stop you catching diseases like polio.

Index

adverts 13,16,45,46
air raid warden 28,33
Anderson Shelter 28,29

Battle of Britain 25,26,27
blackout 28,29,32,25
Blitz, the 27,29
British Commonwealth 50
British Empire 21,50
bombs 21,22,27,28,29,32,34,36,37,44
buses 14

cars 3,11,15,16,28,52,54
Churchill, Winston 24,26
cinema 19,20,34,46,47,48
coal and coal mining 2,3,4,5,6,38-39,43
coronation, the 45,46,50
cotton 3,5,6

'D' Day 36
Depression, the 7,10,21
dole money 8

electricity 5,11,13,39,50
Elizabeth II 45,50
evacuation 22,23

Festival of Britain 43,44
food 8,29,30,31,37,38,39

gas masks 21
General Infantryman (GIs) 36
Germany and Germans 3,21,22,24-28,30,34,35,54
Government posters 23,30,31,40

Haighs, the 2,15,20,28,29,30,32,35,39,41,44,52,54
hiking 20
Hitler, Adolf 21,23,24,25,26,34
holidays 18,20,52,53
Home Guard 25
housing, 3,9,13,41,42,43

immigrants 49,50
insurance stamps 8,40

Jarrow March 9,10,11

liners 17
Luftwaffe 25,26

motorways 52,53

National Health Service, the 40,41
newspapers 45
New towns, the 42,44

Parliament 40
planes 17,25,26,27,28,31,32,35,36,45,53

prefab 41,44
Prime Minister 10, 21,24,26,45

radio 11,18,21,24,25,26,33,34,35,54
railways 4,14,15,20,27,28,39,43,44,51,52,53
rationing 30,31,33,38,39
roads 15,16,17,52
rock and roll 48,49
Royal Air Force 25,26,33

salvage 31
Second World War 2,7,21,36,37,38,39,40,41,43,49,50,51,52,54
shelters 28,29
ships 3,5,6,7,9,17,24,30,49,53
shops 11,12,30,39
sirens 28
slums 9
smog 43,44
soldiers 21,24,32,35,36
Special Constable 32,33
submarines 30

teddy boys 48,50
teenagers 47,48,49
television 18,20,25,46,54
trams 14

Underground, the 14,29
unemployment 6,7,8,9,10
USA 21,30,36,37

women 5,12,32,33,35,54
Women's Voluntary Service 32,33

Acknowledgements

Every effort has been made to contact the holders of copyright material but if any have been inadvertently overlooked the publishers will be pleased to make the necessary arrangements at the first opportunity.

The publishers would like to thank the following for permission to reproduce material.

Arcaid pp12 (top), 19 (bottom). Associated Press p24 (top). BBC Photographic Library p25. Shaun Bresnahan p27 (left). British Library p45 (left). Brooke Bond p46 (right). JR Bubear p12 (bottom). Conservative Party Research Department p7 (left). ET Archive pp11, 18 (right), 30 (left). Mary Evans Picture Library p16 (right). The Ronald Grant Archive p34 (top). Gerald Haigh p2. Hulton Deutsch Collection pp3, 7 (right), 8, 9, 10, 16 (left), 22 (top) 36 (top), 37, 41 (top), 42, 46 (right). Robert Hunt Library p23. The Trustees of the Imperial War Museum, London, Sir Stanley Spencer – Shipbuilding on the Clyde – Riveters (detail) pp6, 28/29 (bottom) 29, 31 (right), 31 (bottom), Dame Laura Knight – Ruby Loftus Screwing a Breech Ring p32 (top right), Clive Upton – Bomb Disposal Bringing up a 250 Kilo Bomb 32 (bottom), 40. © James Walker Tucker Hiking (1936) – Laing Art Gallery, Newcastle upon Tyne (Tyne and Wear Museums) p20. The Board of Trustees of the National Museum and Galleries on Merseyside p17 (right). The National Motor Museum, Beaulieu p52 (top), 52 (bottom left). By permission of the Keeper for the National Railway Museum, York pp4 (top), 14 (bottom), 15, 51 (top). Robert Opie Collection pp13, 22 (left), 28 (right), 30 (bottom), 31 (top left), 33, 34 (bottom), 52 (bottom right). Popperfoto pp4 (bottom), 5, 18 (left), 21, 28 (left), 32 (top left), 35, 38, 41 (bottom), 44, 45 (bottom), 47 (bottom), 48 (top), 49. © RAF Museum reproduced with the permission of Her Britannic Majesty's Stationers p26. Redferns pp48 (right), 54 (top). S&G Press Agency p43 (right). John Sharp p19 (top). Syndication International pp27 (bottom), 51 (bottom). Topham Picture Source pp17 (left), 24 (left), 36 (bottom), 39, 47 (top), 53, 54 (right), 54 (left).

Front cover photographs reproduced with kind permission by: Hulton Deutsch Collection, The Trustees of the Imperial War Museum, London, Moving Images.